Usborne
First Magic Painting
Farm

Designed and illustrated by Emily Beevers

Dip the brush into water. Then, move it across each picture. The paint will magically appear.

Use the flap at the back of the book to stop the water from seeping through to the next page.

A big tractor

A dear little duck

A noisy rooster

A cheery scarecrow

A magnificent turkey

A happy horse

A fluffy hen

A spotted cow

A fuzzy donkey

A perfect pumpkin